The Science of GOO!

Project editor Sarah MacLeod
US editor Megan Douglass
US executive editor Lori Cates Hand
Design Laura Gardner Design Studio, Samantha Richiardi
Illustrators Adam Benton, Peter Bull, Stuart Jackson-Carter,
Jon @ KJA-artists, Arran Lewis, Gus Scott
Jacket designer Akiko Kato
Jacket design development manager Sophia MTT
Production editor Kavita Varma
Senior production controller Meskerem Berhane
Managing editor Lisa Gillespie
Managing art editor Owen Peyton Jones
Publisher Andrew Macintyre
Art director Karen Self
Associate publishing director Liz Wheeler
Design director Phil Ormerod
Publishing director Jonathan Metcalf

Written by Andrea Mills

First American Edition, 2020
Published in the United States by DK Publishing
1450 Broadway, Suite 801, New York, NY 10018

Copyright © 2020 Dorling Kindersley Limited
DK, a Division of Penguin Random House LLC
21 22 23 24 10 9 8 7 6 5 4 3
004–318164–September/2020

A catalog record for this book
is available from the Library of Congress.
ISBN 978-0-7440-2021-2

DK books are available at special discounts when purchased
in bulk for sales promotions, premiums, fund-raising, or
educational use. For details, contact:
DK Publishing Special Markets,
1450 Broadway, Suite 801, New York, NY 10018
SpecialSales@dk.com

Printed and bound in China

For the curious

www.dk.com

CONTENTS

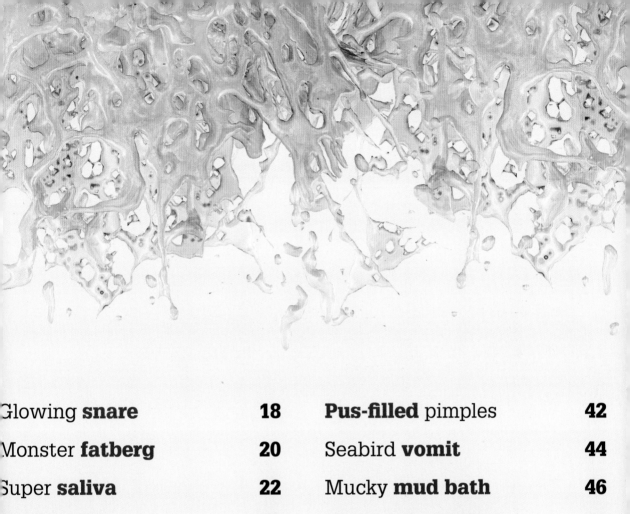

Giant slime

From sticky snot and slimy snail trails to stretchy toy slime and giant fatbergs, goo is found just about everywhere. Whether it is **sticky, slimy, slippery, or sludgy**, goo is fascinating stuff.

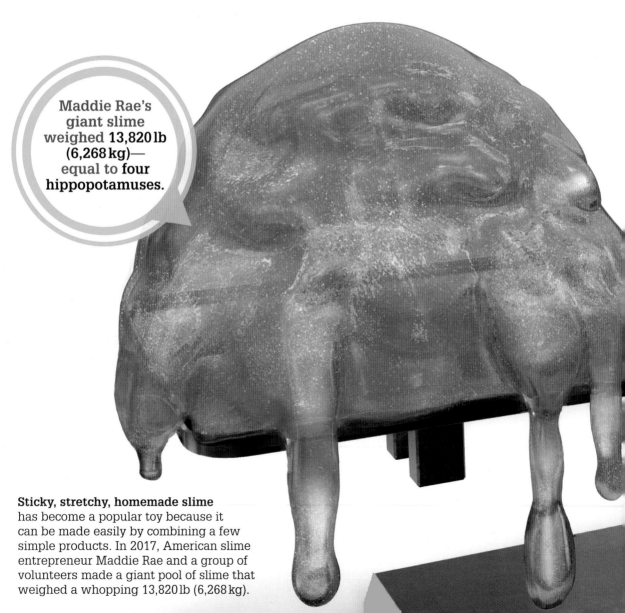

Maddie Rae's giant slime weighed **13,820 lb (6,268 kg)**— equal to **four** hippopotamuses.

Sticky, stretchy, homemade slime has become a popular toy because it can be made easily by combining a few simple products. In 2017, American slime entrepreneur Maddie Rae and a group of volunteers made a giant pool of slime that weighed a whopping 13,820 lb (6,268 kg).

FAST FACTS

Slime requires three key ingredients:

Contact lens solution can be used as an activator.

Activator
(a solution that contains boron)

Water

Craft glue

Craft glue is made up of molecules arranged in long chains that can slide past each other. Adding water helps the molecules slide more easily. When an activator is added, the boron it contains sticks the chains together, turning the mixture into strong, stretchy slime.

Glue and water + Activator → Slime

One female hippopotamus can weigh as much as 3,300 lb (1,500 kg).

PLAYING WITH SLIME

When placed in a container, slime spreads out slowly like a liquid to fill it, but in your hands it can be molded like a solid. Pulling slime quickly makes it break, whereas pulling it slowly keeps it stretchy but intact.

Devil's fingers
fungus

Like fingers sprouting from the ground, these **fiendish fungi** have blood-red tentacles covered in a **dark, foul-smelling goo** that attracts insects.

Native to Australia and now found across Europe and North America, devil's fingers fungi grow from egg-like cases in woodland soil to reveal vibrant red fingers. The dark slime on the fingers contains the seedlike spores needed for new fungi to grow, and has a strong stench of rotting meat. Flies and other bugs are attracted by the smell, eat the slime, and spread the spores in their droppings.

The fungi are also known as **octopus stinkhorns** for their tentacle-like fingers.

New devil's fingers fungi grow from tiny spores. When they land on the ground, the spores grow threads called hyphae, which fuse with other hyphae, feed on the soil, and develop into new fungi.

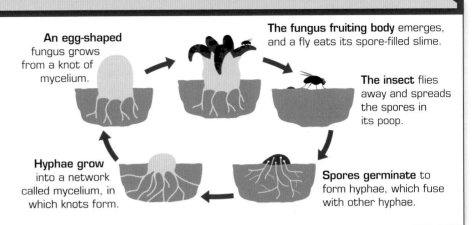

An egg-shaped fungus grows from a knot of mycelium.

The fungus fruiting body emerges, and a fly eats its spore-filled slime.

The insect flies away and spreads the spores in its poop.

Spores germinate to form hyphae, which fuse with other hyphae.

Hyphae grow into a network called mycelium, in which knots form.

Sticky slime may be carried on a fly's body, as well as in its poop, and spread over large distances.

The smelly black goo contains the spores, which will grow into new fungi.

Slippery
frog spawn

Female frogs lay their gooey, jellylike eggs, called frog spawn, underwater. Some species can lay as many as **100,000 eggs in their lifetime.**

GLASS FROGS

Named for their transparent appearance, the glass frogs of Central and South America lay their eggs on leaves. Unlike most other species of frogs, the males guard the eggs from predators that try to eat them. Their glassy skin and eggs make them almost impossible to spot.

Tough, transparent jelly surrounds the embryo, providing protection.

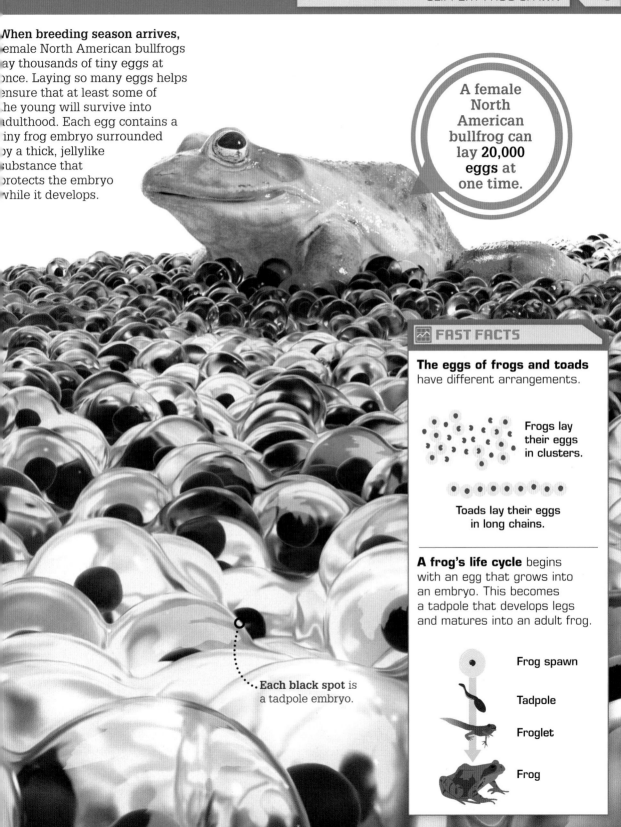

When breeding season arrives, female North American bullfrogs lay thousands of tiny eggs at once. Laying so many eggs helps ensure that at least some of the young will survive into adulthood. Each egg contains a tiny frog embryo surrounded by a thick, jellylike substance that protects the embryo while it develops.

A female North American bullfrog can lay **20,000 eggs** at one time.

Each black spot is a tadpole embryo.

📊 **FAST FACTS**

The eggs of frogs and toads have different arrangements.

Frogs lay their eggs in clusters.

Toads lay their eggs in long chains.

A frog's life cycle begins with an egg that grows into an embryo. This becomes a tadpole that develops legs and matures into an adult frog.

Frog spawn

Tadpole

Froglet

Frog

Slimy **snot**

Grab a tissue! You constantly make gooey gunk in your nose and throat. In fact, each person produces as much as **3.2 pints (1.5 liters) of slimy snot** every day.

The eruption of Mount Vesuvius in 79 CE produced about 1 cubic mile (4 cubic km) of volcanic ash, mud, and rock.

Humans produce **8.9 trillion pints (4.2 trillion liters) of snot every year.**

BIG BLOWHOLE

Whales have huge nostrils, called blowholes, on the tops of their heads. When they surface, whales open their blowholes to breathe and will shoot high plumes into the air made up of water, air, and mucus. When the whales dive back underwater, their blowholes close to stop water flooding in.

The snot produced in your nose and throat is really called mucus. While it may be messy, mucus is essential to survival. It consists mostly of water, but its gooey, sticky consistency protects you by catching any dust, bacteria, and viruses you inhale through your nose. We swallow most of this mucus without noticing.

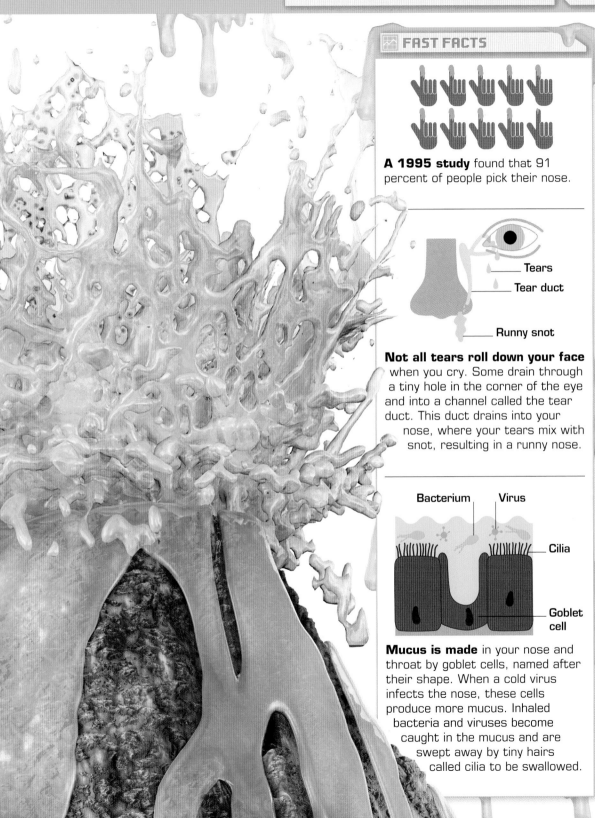

FAST FACTS

A 1995 study found that 91 percent of people pick their nose.

Tears

Tear duct

Runny snot

Not all tears roll down your face when you cry. Some drain through a tiny hole in the corner of the eye and into a channel called the tear duct. This duct drains into your nose, where your tears mix with snot, resulting in a runny nose.

Bacterium   Virus

Cilia

Goblet cell

Mucus is made in your nose and throat by goblet cells, named after their shape. When a cold virus infects the nose, these cells produce more mucus. Inhaled bacteria and viruses become caught in the mucus and are swept away by tiny hairs called cilia to be swallowed.

Nature's
nose pickers

Boogers can block the noses of many animals, not only humans, so our furry friends have had to find some interesting ways to **keep the snot at bay**.

Dogs are known for their wet noses, which are covered with watery mucus to keep them cool and enhance their sense of smell. Their long tongues are perfect for licking away any excess snot that drips from their snouts. ▼

◄ **Buffaloes rely on oxpeckers** to peck dust, dirt, and parasites from their bodies, keeping their skin clean and healthy. These small birds have even been spotted using their beaks to feast on the sticky snot of buffaloes.

As well as long necks, giraffes have long, nimble tongues. This means they can control the tongue muscles to grab and grasp, making their tongues just the tools to reach into the nostrils and lick or push away snot. ▶

Clever chimpanzees use tools for all kinds of work, and nose-picking is no exception. They poke sticks carefully up each nostril to clear mucus, dislodge blockages, and even trigger sneezes that clear the airways. While it may work for chimpanzees, you should not try this yourself! ▼

Giraffes use their **20-in- (50-cm-) long tongues to** dig snot from their noses.

When bonobo babies get blocked up, their mothers pull out all the stops to make them feel better. One female was witnessed helping her offspring to breathe more easily by using her own mouth to suck out the gooey snot blocking her newborn's nostrils. ▼

Like many humans, gorillas stick their fingers up their noses to scrape out boogers, before carefully inspecting any snot they find and eating it. ▶

MARINE MARVEL

The eyes of cuttlefish change shape according to light levels. The pupils take on a unique W-shape in bright light, but become round in darkness. Scientists think cuttlefish adapt their pupils to judge distances with more accuracy, but it may be to keep their eyes camouflaged from predators.

> 80% of the human eyeball is made up of transparent goo.

Squidgy eyeball

Our eyeballs are **fluid-filled organs** that help us see the world. Human eyeballs contain a **thick goo the consistency of egg whites.**

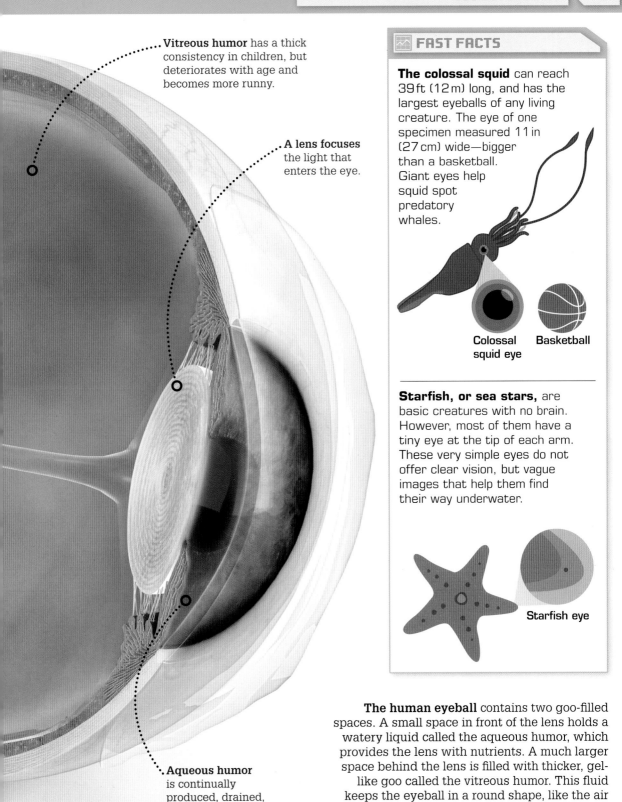

Vitreous humor has a thick consistency in children, but deteriorates with age and becomes more runny.

A lens focuses the light that enters the eye.

Aqueous humor is continually produced, drained, and replaced.

FAST FACTS

The colossal squid can reach 39 ft (12 m) long, and has the largest eyeballs of any living creature. The eye of one specimen measured 11 in (27 cm) wide—bigger than a basketball. Giant eyes help squid spot predatory whales.

Colossal squid eye   Basketball

Starfish, or sea stars, are basic creatures with no brain. However, most of them have a tiny eye at the tip of each arm. These very simple eyes do not offer clear vision, but vague images that help them find their way underwater.

Starfish eye

The human eyeball contains two goo-filled spaces. A small space in front of the lens holds a watery liquid called the aqueous humor, which provides the lens with nutrients. A much larger space behind the lens is filled with thicker, gel-like goo called the vitreous humor. This fluid keeps the eyeball in a round shape, like the air in a soccer ball, and acts as a shock absorber.

Honeydew farming

Ants and aphids have a relationship that benefits both sides—**strong ants protect tiny aphids** in return for the **sweet treat** they produce, honeydew.

SLIMY SYMBIOSIS

Sloths and green algae have a symbiotic relationship. Thick sloth hair provides shelter and water for the slimy algae. In return, the algae give a green tinge to the hair, providing camouflage against the rainforest foliage.

Ants will stop at nothing in their mission to keep aphids close by.

Ants have been known to bite off the wings of aphids in order to stop them flying away.

Chemicals released from the feet of ants leave a trail. The chemicals make the aphids sleepy and slow-moving, so they cannot stray.

Ants will fight off predators, such as ladybugs, that threaten the aphids, making sure their source of honeydew stays safe.

Ants consume the sweet honeydew produced by the aphids.

Stroking the back of aphids stimulates the release of honeydew droplets.

When aphids eat the sap of plants, they produce sugar-rich honeydew as waste. Hungry ants farm colonies of aphids to feast on this waste. In return, ants use their size and strength to care for the aphids and keep attackers away. This is an example of a symbiotic relationship, which brings benefits to both species.

Glowing **snare**

Sneaky New Zealand glow worms secrete **sticky strands of goo** from their mouths before lighting up their bright blue glowing tails. Unsuspecting bugs are attracted to this light and quickly find themselves **stuck in the deadly traps**.

A glow worm's **sticky silk traps** can be as long as 20 in (50 cm).

After hatching inside the Waitomo Caves of New Zealand, these glow worms build tubes of mucus along the cave ceilings and cough up as many as 30 silk threads to hang from them. The glow worms coat these strands with sticky droplets, light their glowing tails, and wait in the darkness for their dinner to arrive.

FAST FACTS

99%
water
——1%
waste

Glow worm glue is almost entirely water. Just 1 percent is made up of bodily waste— salt, protein, and urea (a chemical found in urine).

Glow worms are not the only creatures in the animal kingdom to produce silk:

Weaver ants build nests by connecting leaves with silk.

Silkworms make silk cocoons for their metamorphoses into moths.

Spiders construct silky webs to trap their prey.

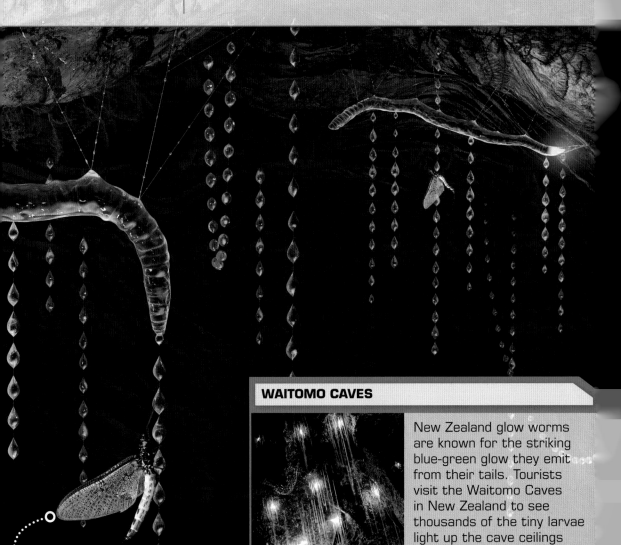

WAITOMO CAVES

New Zealand glow worms are known for the striking blue-green glow they emit from their tails. Tourists visit the Waitomo Caves in New Zealand to see thousands of the tiny larvae light up the cave ceilings like dazzling fairy lights.

This mayfly is stuck in a glow worm's sticky trap.

Monster **fatberg**

In 2017, a **giant fatberg** was discovered lurking in the sewers of London, UK. The **sticky, congealed mass of waste** gave off a disgusting stench and blocked the sewage system.

The London fatberg was 820 ft (250 m) long and weighed 143 tons (130 metric tons). It was made up of cooking oil and animal fat that had combined with solid substances that should not be flushed down the toilet, such as wet wipes and diapers. This mass of sludge hardened and built up over time to form the giant blockage.

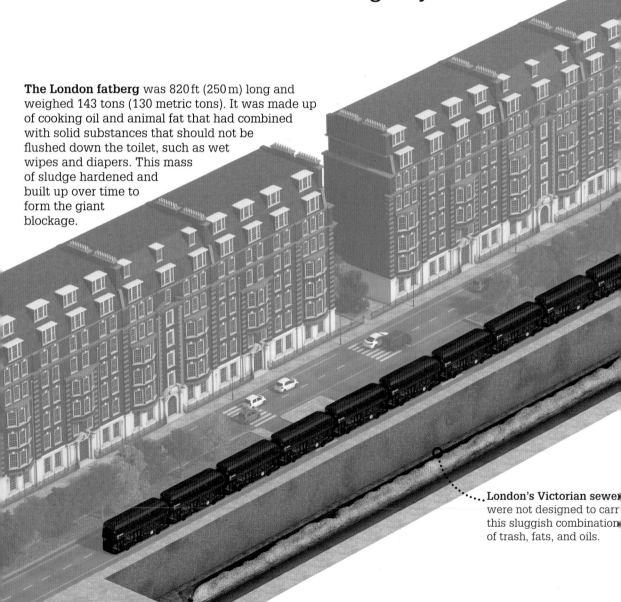

London's Victorian sewer were not designed to carr this sluggish combination of trash, fats, and oils.

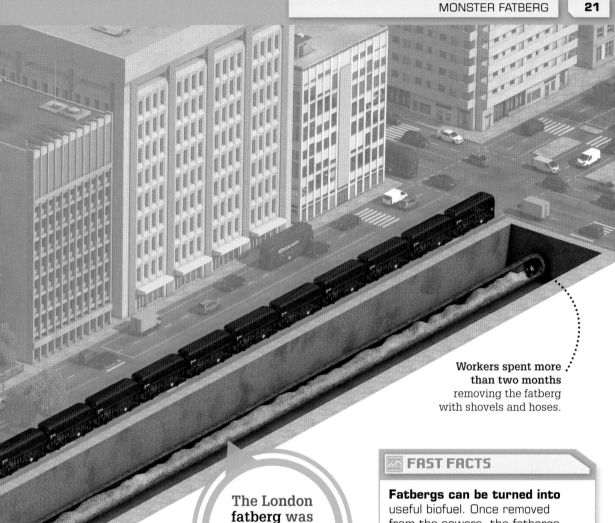

Workers spent more than two months removing the fatberg with shovels and hoses.

The London fatberg was longer than 22 double-decker buses.

FAST FACTS

Fatbergs can be turned into useful biofuel. Once removed from the sewers, the fatbergs are heated to melt down all the oils, fats, and grease to liquid. Unwanted solids and liquids, including water, are extracted, leaving behind a cleaner oil that can be turned into fuel.

FAMOUS FATBERG

In 2018, a sample from the fatberg was put on display at the Museum of London. Flies hatched and mold grew as the toxic piece was prepared for display, and it released the eye-watering stench of a dirty toilet.

Super saliva

Each person produces **1.1–3.2 pints (500–1500 ml)** of saliva every day. The **slimy fluid** performs many important functions to keep your mouth healthy and help you digest the food you eat.

TAKE AIM AND SPIT

Archerfish will spit mouthfuls of water as far as 6.5 ft (2 m) above a river's surface to catch prey. The powerful jets of water knock insects off leaves and branches into the river for the fish to eat.

Your mouth is producing saliva constantly. The slippery slime kills bacteria in your mouth and protects your teeth. When eating, saliva even helps the tongue taste food and gives food a slippery coating that makes swallowing easier. Digestive enzymes in saliva begin the digestion process by starting to break down any food you eat before it travels down to your stomach.

In one week, a person makes enough saliva to fill **30 soda cans**.

Saliva is produced by organs called salivary glands. There are three major salivary glands on each side of your mouth—the parotid gland, the submandibular gland, and the sublingual gland. There are also hundreds of tiny minor salivary glands all around your mouth. All these glands secrete saliva into your mouth through tiny channels called ducts.

Parotid gland

Sublingual gland

Submandibular gland

Saliva is more than **99 percent water,** but also contains mucus, digestive enzymes, and minerals.

Gourmet goo

CASU MARZU CHEESE

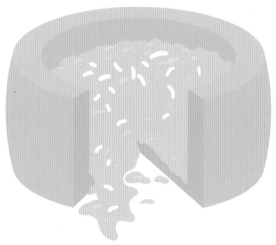

The key ingredient of this Italian cheese is the live larvae of cheese flies. To make it, cheese makers cut a hole in the rind of wheels of sheep's milk cheese so cheese flies can lay eggs inside. When the eggs hatch, the larvae eat the cheese and break it down. Their excretions give the cheese a distinct flavor and soft texture. The average casu marzu contains thousands of the wriggling maggots!

SAGO WORMS

In Southeast Asia, the larvae of sago palm weevils, which grow to around 2 in (5 cm) long, make a tasty meal. They are popular roasted on spits to celebrate special occasions and may even be eaten alive. When served raw, their texture is gooey and creamy.

CAVIAR

Nicknamed "black gold," caviar is considered a true delicacy. These tiny eggs of sturgeon fish make a soft, squidgy goo that melts in the mouth with a fresh but slightly salty flavor. The most prized caviar comes from fish in the cold waters of the Caspian Sea, between Europe and Asia, and sells for a high price in expensive restaurants around the world.

CASTOREUM

Beavers produce a fragrant substance called castoreum that they mix with urine to mark their territory. These secretions may not sound mouth-watering, but were used throughout the 20th century as an additive to sweeten the flavor of some food and drinks. The use of castoreum is now rare, and synthetic flavorings are used instead.

HONEY

Making honey is a sticky business. After honeybees have sucked nectar from flowers, they regurgitate it into the mouths of other bees. The bees transfer it mouth-to-mouth and mix it with digestive enzymes that turn it into tasty honey. This goo is regurgitated into a honeycomb cell, where bees use their wings like a fan to remove excess water and make it even stickier.

BIRD'S NEST SOUP

Swiftlet birds make nests from their own sticky saliva, which hardens in the air. In parts of Southeast Asia, these nests are collected for chefs to dissolve in water to make gloopy bird's nest soup. Although this dish is an expensive and sought-after delicacy in China, the soup can cause allergic reactions. In some areas, the collection of nests has been banned because over-harvesting threatens the species. Governments have put strict regulations in place to reduce the illegal collection and sale of swiftlet nests.

TUNA EYES

Appearing on menus across China and Japan, tuna eyeballs can be boiled in water to give a soft, gooey consistency that allows diners to suck out the insides. The eyeballs are an excellent source of omega-3 fatty acids.

ESCAMOLES

The ancient Aztecs were the first to enjoy escamoles, the edible pupae and larvae of ants. Today, the ant larvae begin their lives growing on the roots of agave plants in the Mexican desert before ending up as a tasty topping for tacos, a popular Mexican street food. Escamoles have a distinctive buttery flavor combined with a soft, gooey texture that is similar to cottage cheese.

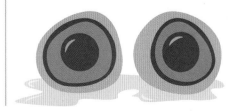

> **Liquefaction can make the ground so gooey it can swallow vehicles.**

📈 FAST FACTS

Liquefaction occurs when waterlogged soil is shaken so much that it loses its strength and stability.

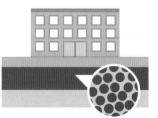

Before an earthquake hits, soil particles are loosely packed together and water fills the small spaces between them.

When shaken, the soil's structure is disturbed and soil particles flow within the surrounding water. The gloopy mixture can no longer support buildings.

Sinking into soil

The full force of an earthquake can shake the ground so much that it **behaves like a thick goo**. Heavy objects may sink as the ground gives way in a process called **liquefaction**.

SHAKEN FOUNDATIONS

The Japanese city of Niigata was hit by an earthquake in 1964, leading to widespread destruction. Liquefaction meant the ground could not support buildings, leading to thousands of homes tilting dangerously and sinking into the ground.

A powerful earthquake struck the city of Christchurch, New Zealand, in 2011. As the earthquake shook the city, the saturated, or waterlogged, ground quickly became a murky sludge. This car was absorbed headfirst into the sludge, but fortunately the driver and their pet dog escaped.

Solid-liquid slime

Not all substances behave how you would expect. **Non-Newtonian fluids** are a group of substances that can **behave like both liquids and solids** depending on how they are treated.

Gooeyoobleck contains long starch molecules (yellow) suspended in water (blue).

The starch and water molecules are able to flow freely past each other when no strong force is applied to the oobleck, so it behaves like a liquid. If you gently insert your hand, it will slide between the molecules.

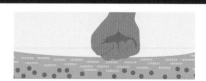

The water molecules are forced aside and the starch molecules stick together to form a temporary solid surface if a sudden force is applied to the oobleck. The oobleck will feel solid if you hit it with your fist.

You can dip your fingers gently into liquid oobleck, just like water, but applying pressure turns the slime solid. ⭘

You can **scoop up** runny oobleck and **squash it into a solid ball.**

Oobleck is a non-Newtonian fluid created by mixing cornstarch with water. Most of the time, oobleck behaves like a typical free-flowing liquid. However, when you scoop it up and squeeze it, oobleck feels solid. If you release the pressure, the oobleck will return to a liquid state and trickle through your fingers.

RUNNING ON SLIME

If you make a pool of oobleck, you could run across it! As your moving feet apply pressure to the fluid, the oobleck will temporarily harden and feel like a solid path beneath your feet. However, you must keep moving—if you stop, the pressure will be reduced and your feet will sink as the oobleck behaves like a liquid again.

Snail trail

Snails may be slow movers, but there is more to these mollusks than meets the eye. Their specialized **silvery slime** allows them to **slide along surfaces and stick to steep walls** with ease.

A snail travels along on a single, muscular "foot" that contracts and relaxes in waves to propel it forward. Glands all over the foot secrete a slimy mucus. This slime is a non-Newtonian fluid (see page 28), which means it behaves like a solid or a liquid under different conditions. As a snail moves, contractions across its muscular foot put pressure on the slime, making it act like a liquid so it can slide along. When the snail stops moving, even up a wall, the pressure is released and the slime solidifies to keep it stuck in place.

The snail moves along by contracting its body in wave motions. When this movement puts pressure on the slime, the slime becomes a liquid and this helps the snail slide along.

Where no pressure is applied because the snail isn't making its muscles contract, the slime becomes more solid and sticky, which helps the snail stay stuck to the surface.

SAFE HAVEN

In warm temperatures, snails survive by withdrawing into their shells for periods known as aestivation. Like hibernation, aestivation is a state of dormancy, or inactivity, that protects animals from hot, dry weather by preserving their energy and water. When they aestivate, snails secrete layers of dried mucus, called epiphragms, that cover and seal the openings of their shells to prevent water loss.

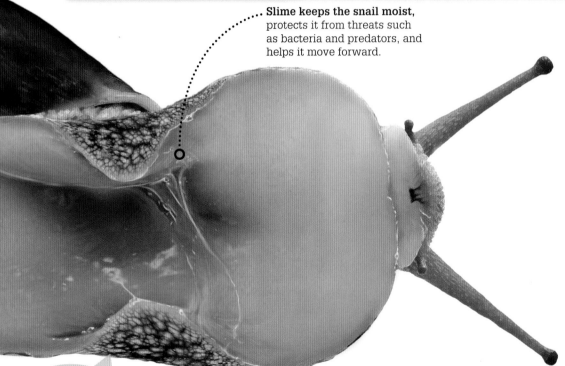

Slime keeps the snail moist, protects it from threats such as bacteria and predators, and helps it move forward.

Glands all over the foot **constantly secrete watery mucus.**

FAST FACTS

Tomato ketchup is another example of a non-Newtonian fluid. Famously tricky to get out of a glass bottle, the thick sauce behaves like a solid most of the time. However, shaking the bottle applies force to the sauce, making it behave like a liquid so it can flow onto a plate.

Tongue **trap**

Frogs have built-in, inescapable traps for catching dinner. Their **super-soft tongues and specialized saliva** work together to grab, grip, and pull in prey.

A frog's tongue is 10 times softer than a human tongue, so it easily wraps around prey upon impact.

Frogs can catch prey in **0.07 seconds**— five times faster than humans blink.

HEAVYWEIGHT TARGETS

Frogs and toads use their impressive tongues to catch large prey up to 1.4 times their own body weight. As well as insects, they may eat mice, bats, and even other frogs.

Frogs have saliva that changes between liquid and solid depending on the pressure applied—it is a non-Newtonian fluid (see page 28). The impact of striking prey makes the saliva on their tongues runnier, allowing it to fully engulf their catch. As their tongues retract, the pressure decreases, so the saliva thickens and keeps hold.

Saliva acts like glue between the frog's tongue and the moth's body.

FAST FACTS

Frogs use a clever trick to separate prey from their sticky tongues. As they swallow, they force their eyeballs downward to put pressure on the prey, which slides the food off their tongues and down their throats.

Mucus bubble

Giant larvaceans are small, solitary sea creatures that inhabit all the world's oceans. They survive by filtering food from the water around them using **delicate bubbles of mucus.**

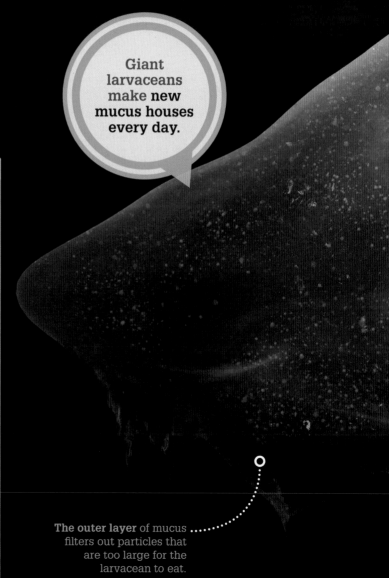

Giant larvaceans make **new mucus houses** every day.

TRANSPARENT TADPOLES

Giant larvaceans can grow to 4 in (10 cm) long, but smaller species of larvaceans may be just 0.4 in (1 cm) long. Their transparent bodies are similar in shape to tadpoles, with tails that propel them through the water. All larvaceans make delicate mucus houses to filter food from the sea water.

The outer layer of mucus filters out particles that are too large for the larvacean to eat.

📊 **FAST FACTS**

Mucus houses gradually become heavy and blocked with the large debris they have filtered from the water. When this happens, larvaceans will leave their houses to swim off and make new ones. The discarded houses, known as "sinkers," drop to the seabed like deflated balloons and become a nutritional food source for deep-sea marine life.

The larvacean is found at the center of the bubble, and it beats its tail to move water through the mucus house.

The inner filter catches smaller, digestible food particles and guides them to the mouth of the larvacean.

Giant larvaceans use sticky mucus to filter food from the sea water Each day they secrete blobs of mucus which they inflate to form mucus houses. These bubbles of mucus can grow to over 3ft (1m) wide. Beating their tails moves sea water through the houses, so particles of food can be filtered out for the larvaceans to eat

Living goo

Slime molds are **brainless but brilliant life-forms**. These **jellylike geniuses** can find food in even the trickiest situations, down to their ability to trace where they have been before.

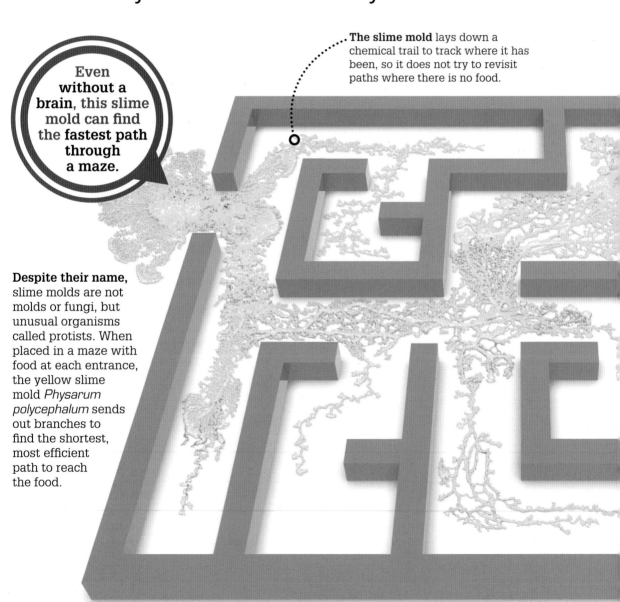

Even without a brain, this slime mold can find the **fastest path** through a maze.

The slime mold lays down a chemical trail to track where it has been, so it does not try to revisit paths where there is no food.

Despite their name, slime molds are not molds or fungi, but unusual organisms called protists. When placed in a maze with food at each entrance, the yellow slime mold *Physarum polycephalum* sends out branches to find the shortest, most efficient path to reach the food.

FOREST SLIME

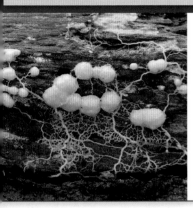

The slime mold illustrated below was tested in a maze, but its usual habitat is damp woodland and forest, where it lives on rotting wood and leaf litter. Slime molds survive and grow by engulfing, and then feasting on, bacteria and fungi.

When the slime mold finds these oat flakes it retracts itself from the paths of the maze where no food has been found and directs its growth toward the food.

More than 1,000 species of slime mold exist around the world in a wide variety of colors, shapes, and sizes. They all look like fungi, but behave more like animals as they move around searching for food.

Ceratiomyxa fruticulosa

Tubifera ferruginosa

Lycogala epidendrum

Fuligo septica

In 2010, a team of researchers placed food around slime mold in locations corresponding to those of cities near Tokyo. They found that the slime's paths closely matched Tokyo's rail system because it seeks the most efficient paths to food, much like transportation designers seek the most efficient routes between cities.

Step 1

Step 2

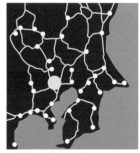

Step 3 The slime mold (yellow) has found the shortest routes between food sources (white).

VOLCANIC WORLD

Io, one of Jupiter's moons, is the most volcanically active world in the solar system, with more than 400 active volcanoes. The most powerful eruptions are visible through large telescopes from Earth.

Lava from Hawaii's Mount Kilauea has reached 2,140°F (1,170°C).

The world's most active volcano is Mount Kilauea in the Hawaiian Islands. Since 1983, Mount Kilauea has been erupting almost constantly. The lava in many volcanoes is sticky and slow. However, the lava from Mount Kilauea comes from molten basalt rock, resulting in a fast-flowing fluid that covers large areas before cooling and hardening.

Liquid rock

Deep beneath Earth's surface lie **chambers of scorching molten rock**. This liquid rock, called magma, can burst through the ground as volcanic eruptions and flow out in unstoppable **rivers of fiery lava**.

FAST FACTS

The color of heated rock can give a good indication of its temperature.

Yellow lava has a temperature of about 1,832–2,192°F (1,000–1,200°C).

Orange lava has a temperature of about 1,472–1,832°F (800–1,000°C).

Red lava has a temperature of about 1,112–1,472°F (600–800°C).

Gooey medicine

YELLOW SOUP

In the 4th century, Chinese doctors cooked the dried poop of healthy people to treat people suffering from diarrhea or food poisoning. Although this yellow soup sounds unappetizing, the idea continues today—patients are sometimes treated with poop transplants from healthy donors.

BEE VENOM

In ancient Greece, the venom of bees was used to treat joint problems and arthritis, as people believed it could reduce pain and swelling. These properties mean that patients in some parts of the world still use it as treatment, despite the potentially harmful effects of venom.

BODY **FAT**

Human fat has been used in medicine for thousands of years. A number of cultures have used fat to treat problems such as gout, broken bones, and open wounds. Animal fat has also come in handy, with goose fat used to soothe sore muscles and goat fat used to calm inflammation.

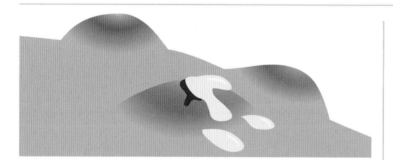

PURGING THE **PLAGUE**

The Black Death, an outbreak of bubonic plague in the 1340s, wiped out half the population of Europe. Symptoms of this dreadful disease included bloody, pus-filled sores on the body called buboes. Although the plague was almost always fatal, doctors tried to save lives by cutting open buboes to drain out the gooey pus.

GLADIATOR BLOOD

Epilepsy is a neurological disorder that causes seizures. Ancient Romans believed drinking the blood of the bravest men was a cure for epilepsy. In ancient Rome, mighty gladiators would fight to the death in arenas to entertain the public. The blood of the dead gladiators would be collected and consumed by epilepsy sufferers.

OOZING OINTMENTS

The ancient Egyptians mixed up odd ingredients to treat eye diseases. Honey blended with pig eyes and tree resin were used to heal eyes. Bats were thought to have good eyesight, so their blood was dropped into human eyes to improve vision. These treatments are not recommended today!

SNAIL SYRUP

In ancient Greece, coughs and sore throats, among other ailments, were treated using the sticky trails left behind by snails. The syrupy mucus was collected and swallowed for instant relief from sore throats and continual coughing. Even in the Middle Ages, a recommended remedy for coughs was snail slime sweetened with sugar.

Pus-filled pimples

Swollen spots appear on the skin when tiny openings called pores become clogged by dead skin cells. **Thick, white pus** slowly builds up inside like volcanoes ready to erupt.

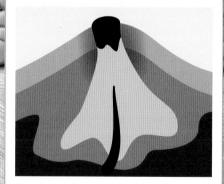

Blackheads are another type of pimple. While whiteheads are sealed off from the air and build beneath the surface, blackheads are pimples that are not sealed off, but open to the air instead. When air reaches sebum clogging up pores, the air reacts with the sebum, turning it darker. This leaves a tiny blackhead visible on the surface of the skin.

PIMPLE POPPING

Popping pimples can be tempting, but this is the worst thing to do. Squeezing spots forces the skin to tear open, which can cause scarring, and forces bacteria deeper into the wound, which can lead to infection.

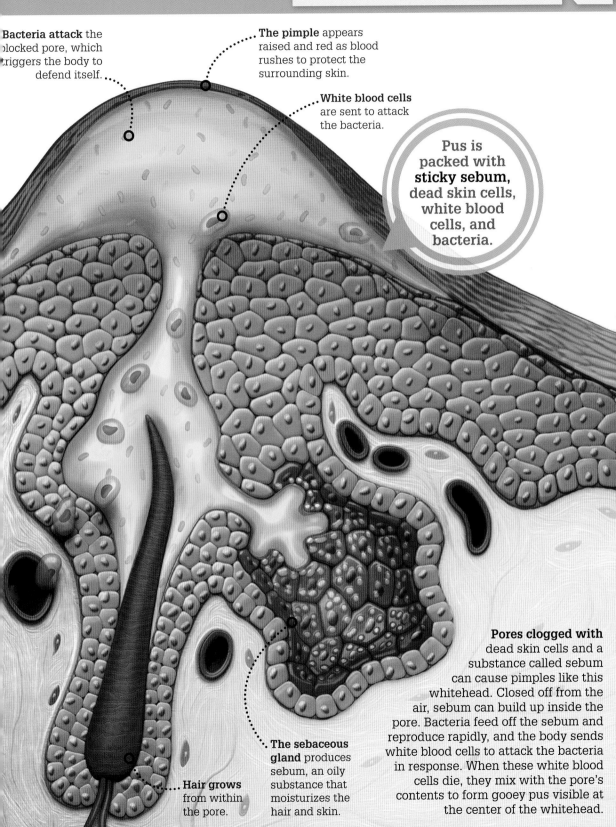

Bacteria attack the blocked pore, which triggers the body to defend itself.

The pimple appears raised and red as blood rushes to protect the surrounding skin.

White blood cells are sent to attack the bacteria.

Pus is packed with **sticky sebum,** dead skin cells, white blood cells, and bacteria.

Hair grows from within the pore.

The sebaceous gland produces sebum, an oily substance that moisturizes the hair and skin.

Pores clogged with dead skin cells and a substance called sebum can cause pimples like this whitehead. Closed off from the air, sebum can build up inside the pore. Bacteria feed off the sebum and reproduce rapidly, and the body sends white blood cells to attack the bacteria in response. When these white blood cells die, they mix with the pore's contents to form gooey pus visible at the center of the whitehead.

Seabird **vomit**

Fulmar chicks may look fluffy and feeble, but these young seabirds have a **secret weapon**. When threatened, they will **shoot smelly, sticky oil** over their attackers.

The name fulmar, meaning "foul gull," refers to the pungent orange oil the birds use as a weapon. Vulnerable chicks store this vile vomit until they need to fire it at predators, such as hungry birds. The sticky goo mats the feathers of intruding birds, and the vile smell deters any other aggressors.

PROTECTIVE PUKE

Vultures are among the few creatures that bring up their food for self-defense. If they feel threatened, they can produce highly acidic, strong-smelling vomit from their stomachs that can sting predators. Vomiting also makes the vultures lighter, enabling them to quickly fly away.

FAST FACTS

— 6 ft (1.8 m) —

Fulmar chicks and adults are able to shoot their smelly stomach oil 6 ft (1.8 m). Adults use the oil as an energy source during long journeys.

Skunks also produce a smelly defensive goo. If threatened, they may shoot a foul-smelling oil from glands under their tail to ward off potential attackers.

Fulmar chicks are covered in soft, downy fluff and cannot take flight until their feathers grow, making them vulnerable to predators.

The oil **sticks like glue** to the wings of predatory birds, so **they cannot fly**.

Mucky mud bath

Bathing does not guarantee squeaky clean results in the animal kingdom. Some animals find themselves in a **mucky mess** instead, after **bathing in pools of sludgy mud.**

Water buffaloes use their horns to churn up the ground into mudholes.

BLOOD SWEAT

Hippopotamuses use a different goo to protect their sensitive skin, known as "blood sweat." They release a thick, red mucus through their pores that acts as a moisturizing sunscreen. It also regulates body temperature and prevents infections.

During the hot summer months, water buffaloes often submerge themselves in mud. They have very few sweat glands and run the risk of overheating, so bathing, or wallowing, in gloopy, wet mud cools them down. It also provides welcome relief from the bothersome bites of mosquitoes and other bugs.

FAST FACTS

Mudholes are wildlife magnets. Even if they are only the size of small puddles, animals will work hard to turn them into massive mud baths.

Elephants roll around in mud and throw it over themselves to cool off and protect their skin from the sun.

Rhinoceroses coat themselves in mud to get rid of parasites. The bugs get stuck in the muck, and the rhinos rub against trees to scrape them off.

Sassabies are African antelopes that perform "mud-packing." Males use their horns to sling mud at other males to establish dominance and territory.

Water buffaloes cake themselves in mud for hours in the daytime to avoid direct sunlight.

When you inhale particles such as pollen, dust, or bacteria, the delicate lining of your nose can become irritated. Triggered by your brain, sneezing is your body's automatic response to get rid of the intruders and try to keep you healthy. Sneezes blast out watery, sticky mucus with explosive force to remove the irritants.

The droplets in sneezes travel at speeds up to **100 mph (160 kph).**

Droplets exit the mouth and nose at the same time, and can reach distances of 26 ft (8 m) away.

High-speed
sneeze

A single sneeze shoots **thousands of mucus droplets** through the air. These droplets can fly out **faster than cars travel on highways**. Bless you!

SPREADING GERMS

Sneezes can contain bacteria and viruses, including the common cold and influenza. Covering your nose and mouth when you sneeze, together with regular hand washing, helps prevent spreading these germs to other people.

Bacteria in a sneeze can stay alive in the air for as long as 45 minutes.

Each slimy droplet of mucus may contain dust, pollen grains, viruses, and bacteria. These particles get trapped in the sticky mucus inside the nose and are removed by sneezing.

FAST FACTS

Sneezing never happens during sleep, because the area of your brain responsible for sneezing shuts down when you are asleep.

The longest ever sneezing fit began in 1981 and lasted 976 days. British schoolgirl Donna Griffiths sneezed about one million times in the first year and continued for almost three years in total.

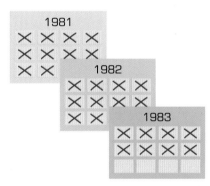

Sneezing is not the only way that humans fire mucus from their bodies at top speed.

Mucus particles released by coughing can travel at 50 mph (80 kph).

While resin is only produced by some trees, sap exists in all plants. Made up of water, sugar, nutrients, minerals, and hormones, sap is a runny fluid that is carried around plants to provide nourishment.

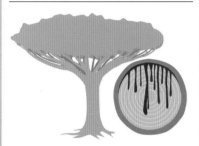

Dragon's blood trees take their name from the red resin that seeps from their trunks and looks like blood. In ancient times this resin was used as medicine, dye, varnish, and incense.

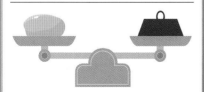

The largest deposits of amber are found in countries around the Baltic Sea. About 110,000 tons of amber were produced in forests there 44 million years ago.

Oozing resin

When attacked by insects or disease-causing microorganisms some trees protect themselves by releasing **a thick goo called resin.** The substance oozes out of trees to seal their trunks against infection and invaders, like scabs forming over wounds.

MAPLE SYRUP

The delicious, sticky syrup that many people pour over their morning pancakes comes from the sap of some maple trees. Syrup harvesters hammer small taps into tree trunks and collect the sap that drips out. The collected sap is heated to concentrate it into sweet syrup.

ome trees, most commonly
onifers, produce gluey
esin. If wounded by fungi
r insects, resin leaks out of
he bark of these trees and
ardens when exposed to
he air, sealing wounds and
reventing further damage.
)ver millions of years, resin
an harden and fossilize to
ecome amber.

A spider
on a tree
can become
**trapped inside
the resin** as it
oozes out.

If buried under the right
conditions, resin may turn
into beautiful orange amber.

History of glue

200,000 YEARS AGO

Neanderthals created the first glue 200,000 years ago by burning the bark of birch trees to extract sticky tar. The adhesive was used to create tools and weapons, such as axes and spears, by gluing stone tools to wooden handles.

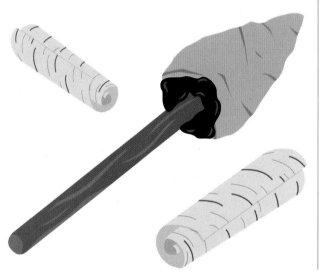

100,000 YEARS AGO

Excavations at Blombos Cave in South Africa revealed how Stone Age people made paint to decorate cave walls, their bodies, or animal skins. Brightly colored pigments from ocher in the ground were blended with gooey animal fat and marrow in the shells of sea snails. The fat may have been added to help the pigments stick to surfaces.

C.4000 BCE

Pottery vessels discovered at ancient burial sites by archaeologists have provided evidence that ancient civilizations repaired objects with simple glues. The broken pots had been repaired using glue made from the naturally sticky sap produced by pine trees.

C. 1323 BCE

Excavations of ancient Egyptian tombs revealed that glues were used in ornate furniture. Artifacts uncovered in King Tutankhamen's tomb used glue made from animal fats to stick thousands of tiny pieces of wood to furniture in decorative patterns.

1942

American researcher Dr. Harry Coover discovered a super sticky goo while working with plastics in World War II, but rejected it for being too sticky. Years later, Coover and his colleague Fred Joyner experimented with the same substance, called cyanoacrylate, and saw its potential as an instant glue that could stick to almost any material. Now known as The Original Super Glue®, cyanoacrylate went on sale in 1958, changing the course of adhesive history.

THE FUTURE OF GLUE

Researchers are now looking to the natural world for adhesive inspiration. Mussels, barnacles, and oysters secrete substances that enable them to hold firmly onto wet rocks. Scientists are trying to replicate this sticky secretion to form a glue that will work underwater for ship repairs. Snail trails are also being studied—scientists are attempting to create a reversible glue that softens and stiffens in the same way as snail slime (see page 30).

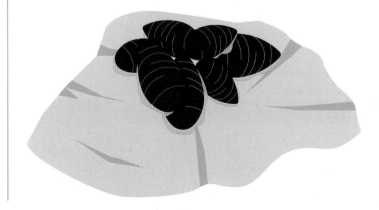

1974

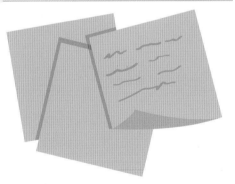

American scientist Arthur Fry was keen to find a way to keep his bookmark in place while singing hymns in a church choir. Remembering that a colleague, Spencer Silver, had created a light adhesive in 1968, Fry used this glue to make small paper notes that were easy to use, could stick temporarily, and could be used repeatedly. Sticky notes like these are now sold around the world.

Flypaper plant

Sundews are pretty plants with big appetites and **can kill insects in minutes**. Attracted by the colors and fragrances of the plants, insects **get stuck in their gluey goo** before being digested slowly.

Sundews can take months to fully digest their prey.

Each tiny tentacle on this leaf is coated in gooey mucilage. This mucilage contains enzymes that will digest any trapped prey.

Sundews are a carnivorous plant species found around the world. They secrete a sweet, gluey substance called mucilage at the tips of their red tentacles to entice and trap passing prey. When insects, like this fly, get stuck in the mucilage on the tentacles, the leaves coil tightly around them. Powerful enzymes in the mucilage slowly digest the prey, and the plants then absorb the nutritious remains

It takes 15 minutes for sundews to kill trapped insects, although the entire digestion process takes much longer.

Sundews are well adapted to attract and capture unsuspecting insects that come too close to their deadly, gooey traps.

A fly becomes stuck in the sundew's gluey mucilage and begins to struggle.

The struggling fly gets stuck to even more tentacles. The leaf begins to wrap around the fly, killing it.

The fly is broken down by the digestive juices in the mucilage and is absorbed by the plant.

Insects are attracted to the sundew's bright colors and sweet scent.

A fly finds itself trapped when it makes contact with the many sticky tentacles.

PITCHER PLANTS

Another type of carnivorous plant, called a pitcher plant, traps prey within deep liquid-filled jugs. Slippery walls stop prey from climbing out, so the goo inside can drown and digest them. Some pitcher plants are large enough to trap small mammals, including mice.

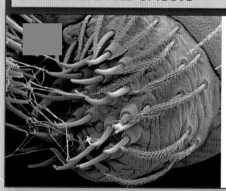

Spiders have silk-spinning organs on their abdomens called spinnerets. Silk threads are pulled through tiny nozzle-like openings on their spinnerets called spigots. The size of these openings can be altered to change the strength, thickness, and texture of the silk as it is pulled through, depending on its purpose.

Sticky silk

The silk secreted by spiders begins as a **thick goo**. As it is drawn out of their bodies, it alters to become sticky, waterproof, elastic, and **tougher than any other natural or synthetic fiber on Earth.**

FAST FACTS

Spiders produce and store silk in silk glands. The gel-like liquid is drawn from the glands through narrow channels, where it is converted to a solid. The silk can then be drawn out as a strong thread through organs called spinnerets. Spiders can have a number of silk glands, and each gland will produce silk with different properties and functions.

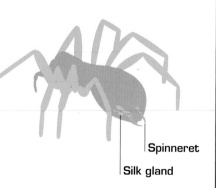

Spinneret

Silk gland

As spiders draw gooey silk out of their bodies, it turns into a solid silk strand in under a second. *Argiope aurantia* spiders from the Americas can produce several different types of silk for different purposes, such as weaving sticky webs, creating sacs to protect their eggs, and encasing prey like this cricket.

Spiders can produce up to **seven different types of silk** to suit a range of uses.

This silk is stretchy and strong, so is used to bind up prey for the spider to eat later.

Silk webs lose their stickiness within a day, so spiders sometimes eat their webs to make use of some of the energy and protein that they contain.

Sea slime

The world's oceans are home to a host of **slime-squirting sea creatures** that have developed ingenious ways of using **goo to get by**.

Sea hares are soft-bodied mollusks found in shallow coastal waters that release toxic clouds of ink to scare and distract predators. The goo includes a sticky mixture of chemicals called opaline. When this opaline sticks to the antennae of attackers, it masks their senses and stops them in their tracks.

Sea cucumbers can **quickly regenerate their sticky organs**.

Shallow Caribbean waters shine at night as little crustaceans called ostracods produce glowing blue mucus. The production and emission of light by living organisms is called bioluminescence. Male ostracods secrete their glowing mucus in courtship displays to attract females. The bioluminescence can also be used to scare away predators.

Jellyfish are unusual animals that have roamed Earth's oceans for more than 500 million years and have survived multiple mass extinctions. The simple, squidgy creatures are 95 percent water and just 5 percent solid matter. Some species can grow to giant sizes—the lion's mane jellyfish can stretch as long as 120 ft (37 m).

Hagfish are eellike marine fish that produce messy mucus to defend themselves from predators. They will release a teaspoon of mucus, which can expand to become 10,000 times larger within a fraction of a second. The stringy goo blocks up the gills and throats of predators, giving the hagfish time to escape.

Parrotfish prepare for sleep by secreting large bags of slimy mucus from glands in their gill cavities to surround their bodies. Scientists are not sure why the fish create these cocoons, but they are thought to protect the fish from tiny parasites and larger predators.

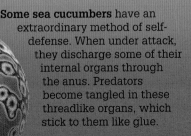

Some sea cucumbers have an extraordinary method of self-defense. When under attack, they discharge some of their internal organs through the anus. Predators become tangled in these threadlike organs, which stick to them like glue.

Blooming goo

Under the right conditions, a type of microscopic bacteria called cyanobacteria can cover huge expanses of water with **gunky green goo** that looks like **giant spillages of pea soup.**

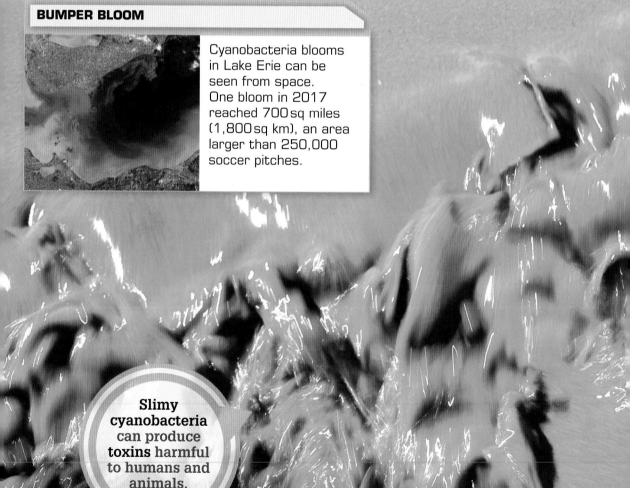

BUMPER BLOOM

Cyanobacteria blooms in Lake Erie can be seen from space. One bloom in 2017 reached 700 sq miles (1,800 sq km), an area larger than 250,000 soccer pitches.

Slimy cyanobacteria can produce **toxins** harmful to humans and animals.

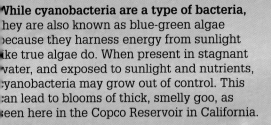

While cyanobacteria are a type of bacteria, they are also known as blue-green algae because they harness energy from sunlight like true algae do. When present in stagnant water, and exposed to sunlight and nutrients, cyanobacteria may grow out of control. This can lead to blooms of thick, smelly goo, as seen here in the Copco Reservoir in California.

Cyanobacteria blooms threaten aquatic life because the bacteria use up much of the oxygen dissolved in the water that animals, such as fish, need to survive.

📈 FAST FACTS

Blooms can be caused by different factors. Some blooms are the direct result of human activity, while others occur naturally.

Farmers use fertilizers to help plants and crops grow. When these substances wash into seas, rivers, and lakes they provide the cyanobacteria with nutrients. The cyanobacteria thrive in the presence of the extra nutrients, leading to blooms.

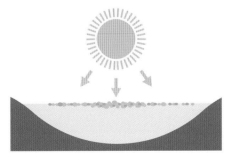

Cyanobacteria thrive in sunshine and warm temperatures. Through a process called photosynthesis, the tiny bacteria get energy from the sunlight and their growth accelerates.

GLOSSARY

Algae
Simple, plantlike organisms that live in water and make their food by photosynthesis.

Archaeologist
A person who studies graves, tools, and other objects to learn about people of the past.

Bacteria
Microscopic, single-celled organisms that make up one of the main kingdoms of life on Earth.

Bioluminescence
The production and emission of light by living organisms.

Camouflaged
Colored, patterned, or shaped to match the surroundings.

Carnivore
A meat-eating animal or plant.

Cell
A tiny unit of living matter. Cells are the building blocks of all living things.

Cilia
Hairlike structures on some cells that sweep substances, such as mucus, along.

Digestion
The process of digesting (breaking down) food.

Embryo
An early stage in the development of an animal or plant.

Enzyme
A substance that organisms produce to speed up particular chemical reactions.

Fossil
The remains or impression of a prehistoric plant or animal.

Fossilization
The process by which plants or animals turn into fossils.

Fruiting body
The part of a fungus that grows above the ground.

Fungus
A type of living organism that is neither a plant or an animal, and feeds off rotting matter.

Gland
An organ in an animal's body, such as the salivary gland, that makes and releases a particular substance.

Hormone
A chemical messenger produced by organisms to control certain life processes.

Larva
The early stage in the life cycle of an animal that undergoes metamorphosis to change into an adult.

Leaf litter
Dead plant material found on the ground.

Metamorphosis
A major change or changes in an animal's body shape during its life cycle.

Microorganism
An organism too small to be seen with the naked eye, such as a bacterium.

Molecule
A tiny particle of matter made up of smaller particles joined together.

Mollusk
A soft-bodied animal, such as a snail or sea hare, that is often protected by a hard shell.

Neurological
Relating to the nervous system, or brain and nerves, of an animal.

Non-Newtonian fluid
A substance that can behave like a liquid and a solid depending on the pressure applied to it.

Parasite
An organism that lives on or inside another organism and feeds from it for an extended period.

Photosynthesis
The process by which plants use sunlight, water, and carbon dioxide to make food.

Pigment
A chemical that gives an object color.

Predator
An animal that hunts other animals for food.

Prey
An animal that is hunted as food by other animals.

Protist
An organism that usually consists of a single cell and is not an animal or plant.

Pupa
The resting stage in the life cycle of an insect that undergoes metamorphosis.

Secretion
A substance produced and secreted (released) by a cell, gland, or organ.

Spore
A microscopic package of cells produced by a fungus or plant that can grow into a new individual.

Stagnant
A word for a body of water that does not move or flow, and can become dirty and foul-smelling.

Toxin
A poisonous substance produced by organisms that can cause diseases.

Virus
A tiny agent that can infect animals, plants, and bacteria and cause illness.

White blood cell
A type of blood cell found in animals that protects the body from infection and disease.

INDEX

ACKNOWLEDGMENTS

Dorling Kindersley would like to thank the following people for scientific consultation: Professor Kathie Hodge, Dr. Jody MacLeod, Mainstone Veterinary Clinic, and Julian Whitehead. The publisher would also like to thank Katie John for proofreading; Helen Peters for indexing; and Tom Bailey, Zaina Budaly, Abigail Ellis, Ben Morgan, and Katie Varney for editorial assistance.

The Original Super Glue® is a Registered Trademark of the Original Super Glue Corporation.

The publisher would like to thank the following for their kind permission to reproduce their photographs:

(Key: a-above; b-below/bottom; c-centre; f-far; l-left; r-right; t-top)

6-7 TurboSquid: 3d_molier International / Dorling Kindersley (Flies). 8 Alamy Stock Photo: Ingo Arndt / Nature Picture Library (clb). 10 Getty Images: Robyn Beck / AFP (clb). 12 naturepl.com: Tui De Roy (bl). 13 Getty Images: Begoa Tortosa / EyeEm (br). naturepl.com: Will Burrard-Lucas (c); Konrad Wothe (bl). 14 Alamy Stock Photo: Charles Stirling (Diving) (tl). 16 Alamy Stock Photo: Gaertner (clb). 19 Alamy Stock Photo: Matej Halouska (bc). 20-21 TurboSquid: RickMcC / Dorling Kindersley (Buildings). 21 Getty Images: Daniel Leal-Olivas / AFP (bl). 22 Alamy Stock Photo: Stephen Dalton / Avalon / Photoshot License (clb). 26-27 Mark Lincoln. 27 Alamy Stock Photo: Historic Collection (crb). 29 Alamy Stock Photo: Paul Biggins (crb). 31 Alamy Stock Photo: Itsik Marom (tl). 33 Alamy Stock Photo: Bruce Davidson / Nature Picture Library (tr). 34 Science Photo Library:

Alexander Semenov (clb). 37 Alamy Stock Photo: Jack Barr (cb); Georg Stelzner / imageBROKER (tl). 38 NASA: JPL / University of Arizona (tc). 38-39 Getty Images: G. Brad Lewis / Aurora Creative. 42 Alamy Stock Photo: Vladimir Gjorgiev (bc). 44 Alamy Stock Photo: Max Allen (bl). 46 naturepl.com: Eric Baccega (bl). 46-47 Getty Images: VCG. 49 Alamy Stock Photo: Science Photo Library (tl). 50 Alamy Stock Photo: Marc Bruxelle RF (bc). 51 Alamy Stock Photo: Dmitry Gool. 55 Dreamstime.com: Chi Keung Chan / Waterfallbay (bc). 56 Science Photo Library: Steve Gschmeissner (tl). 60 Alamy Stock Photo: NASA Image Collection (cl). 60-61 Alamy Stock Photo: David McLain / Aurora Photos / Cavan

All other images © Dorling Kindersley
For further information see: www.dkimages.com